This book belongs to:

. . . .

Inside your *On The Plane Sticker Activity Book*, there are lots of fun things for you to do as you fly off on your journey! Use felt-tip pens to doodle and colour, but don't forget to leave them to dry to make sure they don't smudge. You'll find all the stickers you need to finish the pictures in the middle of the book.

Have fun!

Scholastic Children's Books,
Euston House, 24 Eversholt Street,
London NW1 1DB, UK

A division of Scholastic Ltd
London ~ New York ~ Toronto ~ Sydney ~ Auckland
Mexico City ~ New Delhi ~ Hong Kong

Edited by Jen Wainwright

Published in the UK by Scholastic Ltd, 2014

Illustrated by Samantha Meredith
© Scholastic Children's Books, 2014

ISBN 978 1407 14254 8

Printed in Malaysia.

2 4 6 8 10 9 7 5 3

Papers used by Scholastic Children's Books are made from woods grown
in sustainable forests.

Off We Go!

Today's the day. Jake and Emma are going on holiday and they're so excited! Use the stickers in the middle of the book to dress them up and get them ready to go.

Passports Ready?

Jake, Emma, Mum and Dad are nearly ready to go to the airport, but they need to make sure they've packed their passports. Look at Emma and Jake's passports, then use felt-tip pens to fill in your own at the bottom of the page.

Name: Jake Jones

Age: 7 1/2

Address: 33 Love Lane, Little Town

Name: Emma Jones

Age: 6

Address: 33 Love Lane, Little Town

At the Airport

It's crowded at the airport, everyone is looking forward to flying off on holiday. Use stickers to add more excited people. Can you unscramble the letters on the board and work out where the planes are going?

DEPARTURES

DESTINATION	FLIGHT TIME	CHECK IN ZONE
1. RASIP	13:20	A – E
2. WEN ROYK	13:35	A – C
3. YDYNES	13:45	H
4. REBNIL	13:50	B – G
5. SOL LAGNEES	14:00	A – C
6. IRO ED NEJARIO	14:05	J – K

Lots of Luggage

Behind the check-in desks, everyone's bags are put on moving belts and taken to the plane. Use stickers to add lots more cases, bags and boxes to the belts.

CHECK IN

Shopping Spree

Mum has asked Emma and Jake to help her buy some presents from the airport shop. Can you find all the items on her list? Mark each one with a sticker when you find it.

MUM'S LIST

A pink bottle of perfume

A new camera

Two teddy bears

A jar of blue sweets

A yellow T shirt

A gold watch

On the Runway

Planes taking off, planes coming in to land – it's always busy at the airport. Use stickers to add some cool decorations to the planes on the runway.

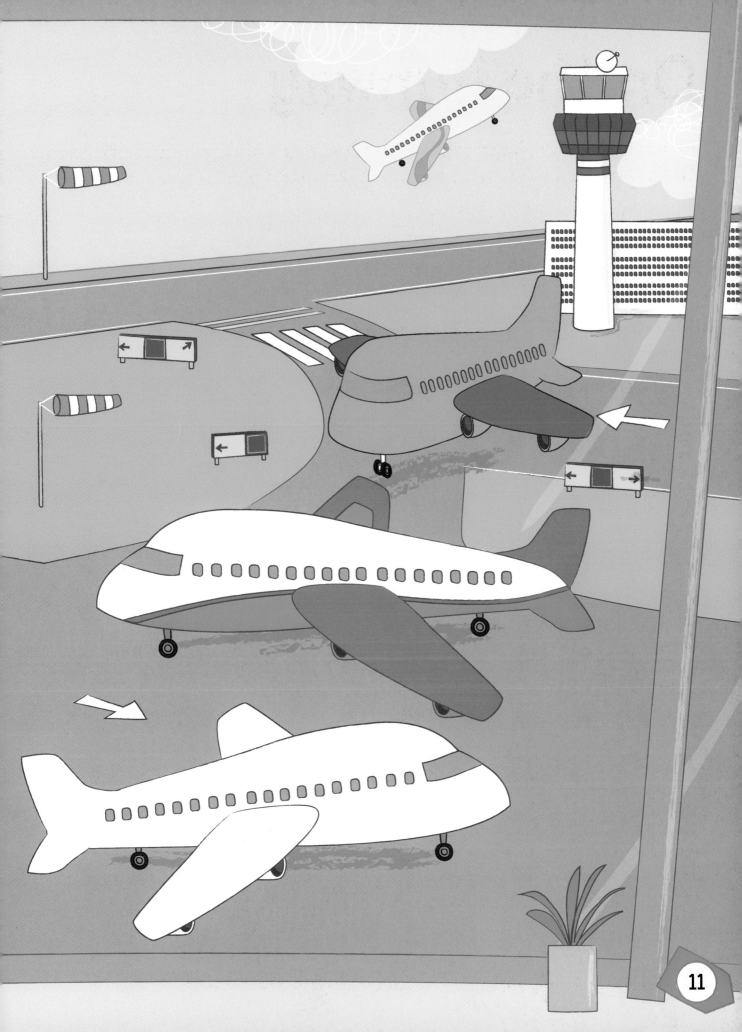

Plane Spotting

Dad says that the plane they'll be taking off in has a red nose on the front, a five-pointed star on the tail, square windows and no propeller. Can you circle the right one?

Final Call

It's almost time to get on the plane and fly away on holiday. Follow the tangled lines to work out which gate Mum, Dad, Emma and Jake need to go to to get on their flight.

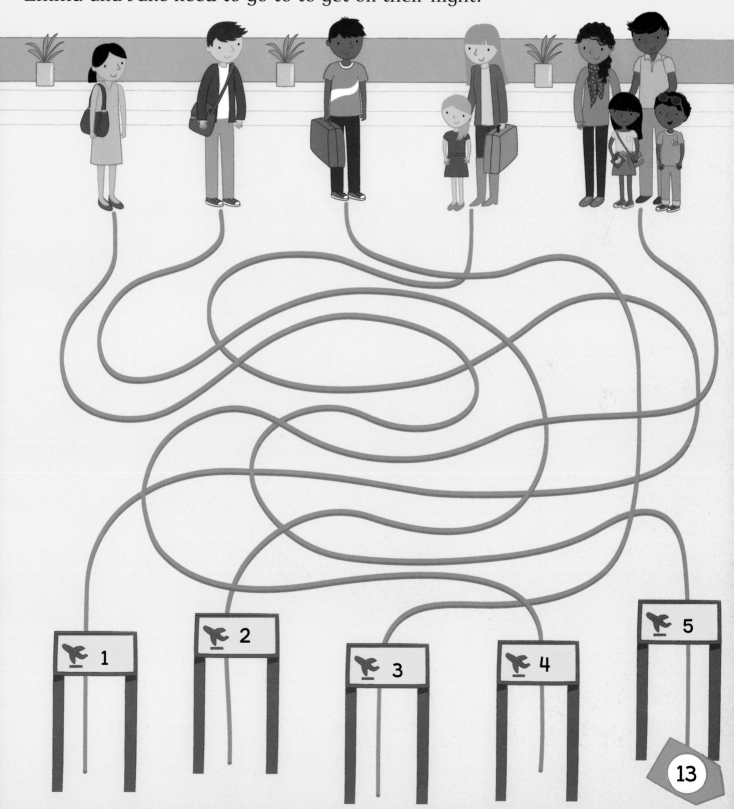

Get Creative

This is Captain Edwards, the pilot, and his team of cabin crew. Use felt-tip pens and stickers to decorate and complete their uniforms so they'll look stylish in the sky.

Time for Take-off

This is the cockpit. It's where Captain Edwards sits to fly the plane. Use stickers to complete the cockpit with dials, levers and buttons, and get the plane ready for take-off.

Up in the Air

Use felt-tip pens to doodle the view from the plane window.
Can you see clouds or birds? What is the weather like?

How Puzzling

The Captain has left you a special secret message. Each letter of the message has jumped forward two places in the alphabet. Can you crack the code?

YGNEQOG CDQCTF!

YG JQRG AQW JCXG C HWP HNKIJV.

Colour in each suitcase green, each backpack red and each plane blue.

Captain Edwards has given Emma and Jake a cool puzzle book to keep them busy on their journey. Can you help them with this puzzle page?

Can you complete the puzzle so that a plane, a bird, a cloud and a suitcase each appear only once in every row, column and group of four squares?

Dinner in the Sky

It's time for some tasty food. Use your stickers to fill the trays with a delicious dinner for Emma and Jake. Yum!

Where Are You Going?

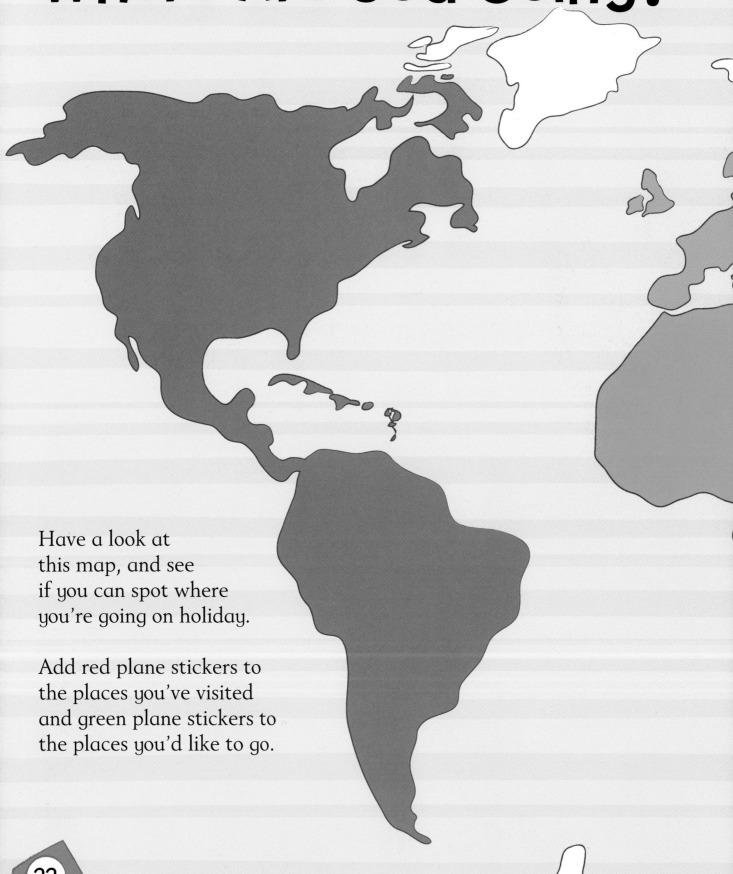

Have a look at
this map, and see
if you can spot where
you're going on holiday.

Add red plane stickers to
the places you've visited
and green plane stickers to
the places you'd like to go.

22

Spot the Difference

Can you spot eight differences between the two scenes?

Ready for Landing

Emma and Jake are amazed at how tiny everything looks from the air! Use stickers and felt-tip pens to finish the scene as the plane comes in to land.

A Big Bag Mix Up

Everyone's trying to find their luggage, but it's all in a bit of a muddle. Can you help the passengers out, and work out which bag each person is looking for?

A

B

C

28

Almost There

Emma, Jake, Mum and Dad can't wait for their holiday to start. Help them find their way to the Seaside Hotel, then use felt-tip pens to colour in the beach scene.

All the Answers

Pages 4-5 At the Airport

1 – Paris   4 – Berlin
2 – New York   5 – Los Angeles
3 – Sydney   6 – Rio De Janeiro

Pages 8-9 Shopping Spree

Page 12 Plane Spotting

Plane 6 is the right plane.

Page 13 Final Call

The family need to go to Gate 4.

Pages 18-19 How Puzzling!

The code reads: Welcome aboard!
We hope you have a fun flight.

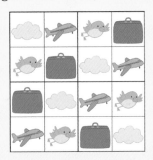

Pages 24-25 Spot the Difference

Pages 28-29 A Big Bag Mix Up

A –   D –

B –   E –

C –   F –

Pages 30-31 Almost There

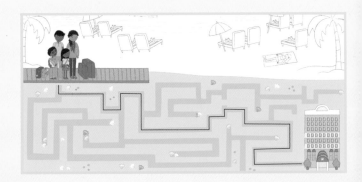